handball-uebungen.de
Trainingseinheiten und Übungen für Ihr Training!

I0220849

Table of contents:

Introduction

Publishing Information
1st English edition released on 18 Oct 2018
German original edition released on 23 Feb 2016

Published by DV Concept
Editors, design, and layout: Jörg Madinger, Elke Lackner
Proofreading and English translation: Nina-Maria Nahlenz

ISBN: 978-3-95641-232-5

This publication is listed in the catalogue of the **German National Library**. Please refer to http://dnb.de for bibliographic data.

Introduction

Dear reader

Thank you for choosing a book of the handball-uebungen.de training guide series.

The five training units in this book focus on training of handball basic skills for young players aged 9 to 12 years. The individual training units deal with passing precision, shooting movements, dribbling technique, breaking away from man coverage, and passing feints, respectively. The players develop the individual skills methodically and step by step from basic to complex level. You may adjust the complexity of the exercises to your team's level of performance by intensifying the individual drills.

This book contains the following training units:

TU 1 – Improving passing precision during running movements (⭐)

The objective of this training unit is to improve the passing precision during running movements, in particular. Following warm-up consisting of combined running moves and passing variants and a short game, the players practice passing while running at full speed during the ball familiarization phase. The goalkeeper warm-up shooting and the subsequent series of shots also focus on playing passes while running at full speed. A second series of shots combines double passes on a defined running path with quick passes in direction of the goal. Finally, the players practice playing precise passes under pressure in a small group game and a closing game.

TU 2 – Developing and improving the shooting movement (⭐)

This training unit focuses on acquiring and improving correct shooting movements. This means shooting while standing and shooting while running, without a jump however, in order to highlight arm and body movements. Following a warm-up exercise which already involves shots, the players practice the shoulder and arm rotation for shooting and subsequently combine these moves in a passing competition. In a short game, the players implement the shooting movements in a game situation. This is followed by the goalkeeper warm-up shooting and a closing series of shots which focuses on shooting at the goal.

TU 3 – Improving the dribbling technique while observing the game situation (⭐)

The objective of this training unit is to improve the dribbling technique focusing on simultaneous observation of the game situation. The players combine movements with dribbling already during the warm-up exercise; in a sprint contest and a short game, they practice dribbling at increased speed. Following the goalkeeper warm-up shooting, there will be a series of shots with additional coordination tasks in which the simultaneous observation of signs will be added. The subsequent small group exercise demands observation of the game situation while dribbling the ball. In a closing game, the players should implement what they practiced before.

TU 4 – Breaking away from man coverage using running feints (⭐)

This training unit focuses on breaking away from man coverage without a ball, by means of running feints. Following warm-up, a sprint contest with changes of direction, and a team ball variant, the players practice quick changes of direction one more time during the goalkeeper warm-up shooting exercise. Subsequently, there will be an individual offense exercise focusing on breaking away by means of running feints. The players will further elaborate this topic in two small group exercises and finally implement what they practiced before in free play.

TU 5 – Gaining positional advantage using passing feints (⭐)

The key topics of this training unit are passing feints and how to combine them with a breakthrough or a return pass to a teammate. Following a warm-up running exercise, the players already learn how to pass the ball cleverly in a short game; this will be further developed in the ball familiarization phase. In the goalkeeper warm-up shooting exercise, the players practice passing feints in combination with a 1-on-1 breakthrough; in the subsequent series of shots, they combine the passing feint with a return pass to their teammate. Both variants will be implemented twice in the subsequent 1-on-1, 3-on-2, and 4-on-4 games.

Training unit requirements:

⭐	Simple requirement (all youth and adult teams)
⭐⭐	Intermediate requirement (youth teams under 15 years of age and adult teams)
⭐⭐⭐	Higher requirement (youth teams under 17 years of age and adult teams)
⭐⭐⭐⭐	Highest requirements (competitive area)

1. Insight into the annual schedule

Annual schedule

The following points should be taken into consideration when creating your annual schedule:

-   How many training units do I have (do not forget vacations, holidays, and the season schedule)?
-   What do I want to achieve/improve this season?
-   What goals should be achieved within a given concept (of the club, the association or federation)?
-   What skills does my team have (do the individual players have)? You should continuously analyze and document the skills of your team so that you can make a target-performance comparison at a regular basis. The level of performance especially varies among young players. This has to be taken into consideration when training these teams. By making well-matched groups, you can optimize the performance of individual players in group training. You may also incorporate your own training units for certain performance groups or players with similar deficits in the annual schedule.

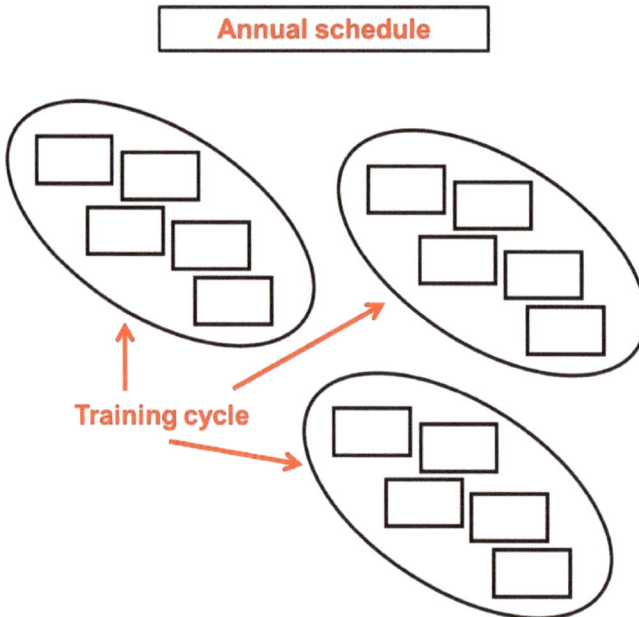

Annual schedule

Training cycle

Individual steps of the annual schedule:

- You may divide your annual schedule into special subsections.
- In the training of a youth team, you might want to apply the following structure:
  o End of season to summer vacations
  o Training during the vacations
  o Phase until beginning of next season
  o You may want to divide the season into a first and a second half (still keeping the vacations in mind).

You should then refine and elaborate these training phases step by step.

- Division of training phases into sections with part-specific objectives (monthly schedule, e.g.)
- Division into weekly schedules
- Planning of individual training units

The present training units are especially suitable for the preparation periods, but also for longer breaks between matches during the season.

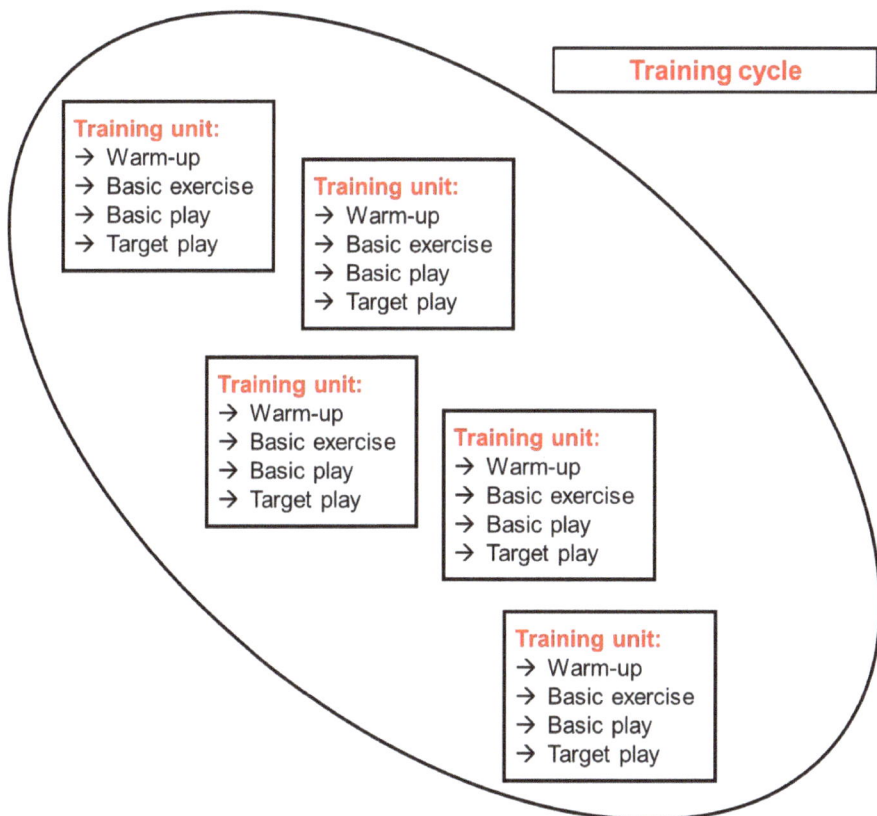

Training cycle

Training unit:
→ Warm-up
→ Basic exercise
→ Basic play
→ Target play

Training unit:
→ Warm-up
→ Basic exercise
→ Basic play
→ Target play

Training unit:
→ Warm-up
→ Basic exercise
→ Basic play
→ Target play

Training unit:
→ Warm-up
→ Basic exercise
→ Basic play
→ Target play

Training unit:
→ Warm-up
→ Basic exercise
→ Basic play
→ Target play

Creating well-structured training units

A clear structure is important for the annual schedule as well as for the planning of the individual training units.

- Work with parts (see monthly schedule). You should work on a special topic over a certain period of time, especially in the training of youth teams. That way, you can repeat exercises and make sure the players memorize the courses.
- Each training unit should have a clear training focus. Do not mix topics within a training unit, but make sure that each exercise has a well-defined objective.
- The players are corrected in accordance with the training unit's focus (when training the defense, defense actions are corrected and pointed out).

2. Structuring a training unit

The focus of the training should run like a red thread through the entire unit. It is advisable to follow the basic timescale below:

- Approx. 10 (15) minutes – warm-up.
- Approx. 20 (30) minutes – basic exercises (2 to 3 exercises max. plus goalkeeper warm-up shooting).
- Approx. 20 (30) minutes – basic play.
- Approx. 10 (15) minutes – target play.

1st timescale for a 60-minute training unit / 2nd timescale in brackets for a 90-minute training unit.

Warm-up practices

- Opening of the training unit: It may be advisable to start the training unit with a ritual (get together in a circle, exchanging high-fives) and to explain the contents and the objectives of the training unit to the players.
- Basic warm-up: Jogging, activation of blood circulation and the musculoskeletal system.
- Stretching/strengthening/mobilization: Preparing the body for the physical stress of the training unit.
- Short games: These should already focus on the objective of the training unit.

Basic exercises

- Ball familiarization (focused on the objective of the training unit).
- Goalkeeper warm-up shooting (focused on the objective of the training unit).
- Individual technique and tactics training.
- Technique and tactics training in small groups.

In general, the running and passing paths are predefined during the basic exercises (you may increase and vary the requirements during the course of the exercise).

Additional information on basic exercise
- Each player should do the drill (switch quickly).
- Very frequent repetitions.
- The players should rotate or do the drill on both sides simultaneously / slightly delayed to avoid long waiting periods.
- Practice individually (1-on-1 to 2-on-2 max.).
- Add additional tasks/drills, if applicable (to make the exercise more complex).

Basic play
Most of all, the basic play differs from the basic exercise in such a way that now there are several **options for action** (decisions). The player(s) should realize the respective options and make the correct decision. Here, the players practice decision-making in particular.
- The players should now implement what they practiced during the basic exercises under **competitive conditions**.
- Working with alternative actions – practicing the decision-making process.
- The players should repeat the drill frequently and try out different actions.
- Working in small groups (3-on-3 to 4-on-4 max.).

Target play
- The players now implement what they practice before in free play. To increase their motivation, you may award additional points or additional attacks for correct implementation.
- In the target play, the players implement what they practiced before (5-on-5, 6-on-6).

Depending on the contents and the objectives of the training unit, you may have to slightly adjust the timescales of the basic exercise and basic play.

Choose topic of training unit:
→ Red thread

Warm up:
Time:
- approx. 10 (15) minutes

Practices:
- "Playful warm-up"
- Games
- Coordination runs
- (Stretching and strengthening)

Basic exercise:
Time:
- approx. 20 (30) minutes

Characteristics:
- Individual/Small groups

Practices:
- Exact instructions re. course of the exercise
- Variants with exact instructions re. the course
- From simple to complex
- No waiting periods for players

Basic play:
Time:
- approx. 20 (30) minutes

Characteristics:
- Small groups

Practices:
- Exact instructions re. course
- Competition

Target play:
Time:
- approx. 10 (15) minutes

Characteristics:
- Team play (small groups)

Practices:
- Free play with the contents of the basic exercise and basic play
- Competition

3. Roles/tasks of the coach

It is mainly the personality and the behavior of the coach that makes the training a success. Therefore, it is important to observe certain behavioral rules to guarantee a successful training. The coach's social skills have an impact as important as his expertise. Especially when training youth teams, the coach serves as a role model and may influence the development of the young players.

A coach should:
- describe the training and its objectives to his team at the beginning of the training unit.
- always speak loud and clear.
- talk from such a position that all players can hear his instructions and corrections.
- recognize and correct mistakes and give advice when correcting.
- mainly correct what is part of the training objective.
- point out and compliment on individual progress (give the player self-confidence).
- support and permanently challenge the players.
- always be a role model – during training and games, but also outside the court.
- come to training and games well-prepared and in a timely manner.

Especially when training youth teams:
- The coach should react to different physical preconditions. This is especially important when training athletics. The difficulty level should always match the players' level of performance. For heterogeneous groups, you might have to present a less difficult version for physically weaker players.
- Motivate the players to hang in, even if they face certain difficulties in the beginning.

4. Training units

No.: 1	Improving passing precision during running movements	☆	90

Opening part		Main part			
X	Warm-up/Stretching		Offense/Individual		Jumping power
	Running exercise	X	Offense/Small groups		Sprint contest
X	Short game		Offense/Team		Goalkeeper
	Coordination	X	Offense/Series of shots		
	Coordination run		Defense/Individual	**Final part**	
	Strengthening		Defense/Small groups	X	Closing game
X	Ball familiarization		Defense/Team		Final sprint
X	Goalkeeper warm-up shooting		Athletics		
			Endurance		

Key:

✗ Cone

△1 Attacking player

●1 Defense player

Large vaulting box

Ball box

Small vaulting box

Small vaulting box, upside-down

Equipment required:
→ 2 large vaulting boxes, 2 small vaulting boxes,
9 cones, ball box with sufficient number of handballs

Description:
The objective of this training unit is to improve the passing precision during running movements, in particular. Following warm-up consisting of combined running moves and passing variants and a short game, the players practice passing while running at full speed during the ball familiarization phase. The goalkeeper warm-up shooting and the subsequent series of shots also focus on playing passes while running at full speed. A second series of shots combines double passes on a defined running path with quick passes in direction of the goal. Finally, the players practice playing precise passes under pressure in a small group game and a closing game.

The training unit consists of the following key exercises:
- Warm-up/Stretching (individual exercise: 10 minutes/total time: 10 minutes)
- Short game (15/25)
- Ball familiarization (10/35)
- Goalkeeper warm-up shooting (10/45)
- Offense/Series of shots (10/55)
- Offense/Series of shots (15/70)
- Offense/Small groups (10/80)
- Closing game (10/90)

Training unit total time: 90 min.

No.: 1-1	Warm-up/Stretching	10	10

Course:
- The players each get a number which they should memorize.
- The players crisscross the entire half of the court and pass a ball in the given order (1-2-3-4... – the last player passes back to 1).
- After a while, the players get a second ball (of another color/design) which must be passed in the same order, as a bounce pass, however.
- After a while, the players get a third ball (of another color/design) which must be passed in the same order, with both hands over the head, however.
- Once coach whistles, the passing order is reversed.

Afterwards, the players perform stretching/mobilization exercises together.

No.: 1-2	Short game	15	25

Setting:
- Position two large vaulting boxes diagonally and use cones to define the shooting line.

Course:
- Two teams play against each other.
- By playing quick passes (A and B) and moving in a well-coordinated manner (C), the team in ball possession tries to put a player in a good shooting position (D).
- The team scores if the shooting player hits one side of the vaulting box.
- The shooting player and the defending players are not allowed to step into the defined area around the vaulting box.
- Following each shooting attempt, the other team gets the ball and starts an attack on the opposite vaulting box.
- As soon as one of the teams has scored two (three) times, remove one of the intermediate parts of the vaulting box.
- The team that takes down their vaulting box first wins the game.

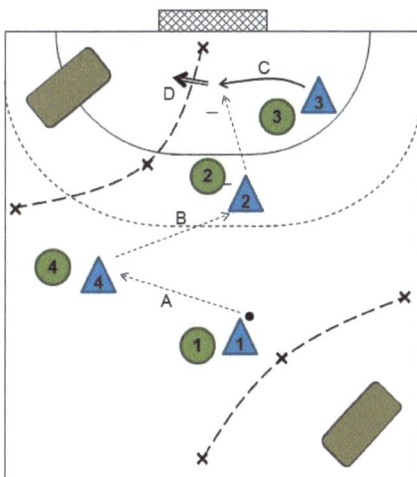

⚠ Following a shooting attempt, the players should adjust immediately and start an attack on the opposite vaulting box.

No.: 1-3	Ball familiarization	10	35

Setting:

- Position a ball box with lots of handballs on the center line and an empty ball box on the goal line.
- Define the feeding/receiving positions with cones.

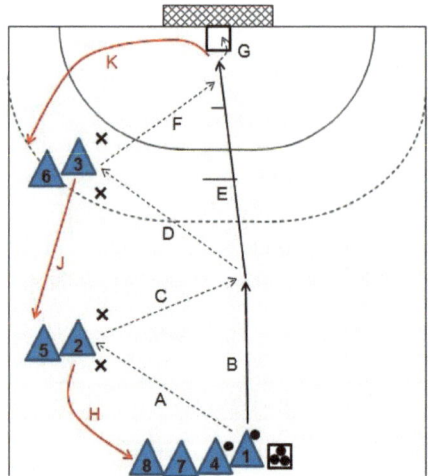

Course:

- **1** passes to **2** (A), starts to sprint (B), and receives a return pass into his running path (C).
- Without slowing down, if possible, and within a three-step limit (no dribbling), **1** passes the ball to **3** (D).
- **1** keeps on running (E), receives a return pass (F), and puts the ball into the empty ball box (G).
- **2** lines up behind **8** (H) after the return pass (C), **3** lines up behind **5** (J) after the pass (F), and **1** lines up behind **6** (K) after putting the ball into the box (G).
- As soon as **3** passes the ball back to **1**, **4** starts the course with a pass to **5**.

⚠ The players should increase their speed gradually over several rounds and catch and pass the ball while running. If applicable, stop the time in the second round and define a target time, i.e. specify how much faster (seconds) the players should do the third round.

No.: 1-4	Goalkeeper warm-up shooting	10	45

Course:

- 2 passes the ball to 1 (A) and receives a return pass (B).
- 2 shoots at the goal as instructed (hands, top, bottom) (C).
- Afterwards, 3 starts the same course.
- The players shoot at the right and left side of the goal alternately.
- Change the feeder/receiver after each round.

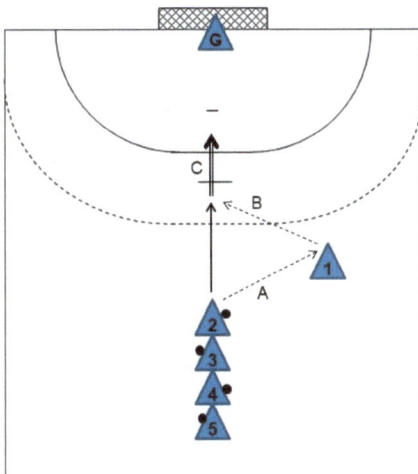

⚠ The passes should be played in such a way that there is a smooth rhythm for the goalkeeper.

No.: 1-5	Offense/Series of shots	10	55

Setting:
- Define the starting positions with cones.

Course:

- 1 starts to sprint without a ball (A) and receives a pass from 2 into his running path (B).
- While running, 1 passes to 3 (C).
- 1 keeps running towards the goal (D), receives a return pass from 3 (E) into his running path, and shoots (F).
- As soon as 3 passes to 1 (E), 2 starts the course on the other side (G) with a pass from 5 and a double pass with 4.
- Change both feeders/receivers after a full round.

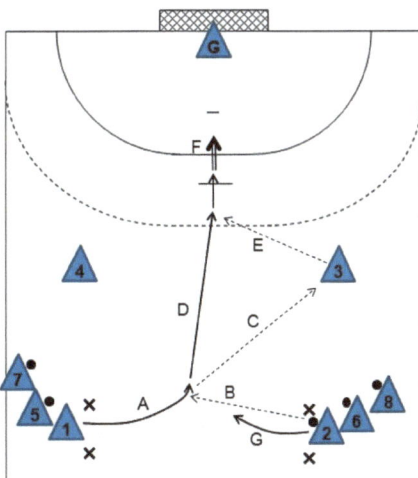

⚠ The players should catch the ball while running and immediately (max. three steps) pass it to the next player.

No.: 1-6	Offense/Series of shots	15	70

Setting:

- Use two cones to define each running path (it should form an "8").
- Put two more cones on the floor to define the running path for the subsequent action (see figure).

Course:

- ▲1 and ▲2 start simultaneously; their running path around the two cones should form an "8" (A).
- While running, they alternately play double passes (B and C) with the feeders/receivers (▲3 and ▲5, ▲4 and ▲6, respectively).
- When the coach whistles, ▲1 and ▲2 run around the cones in the back without a ball (D).
- The coach passes a ball to one of the players (E). ▲1 and ▲2 keep running towards the goal and pass to each other (F) until one of them is in shooting position (G).
- As soon as the coach has whistled, one feeder/receiver each starts running the "8 path". A new player becomes the second feeder/receiver and the course starts over.

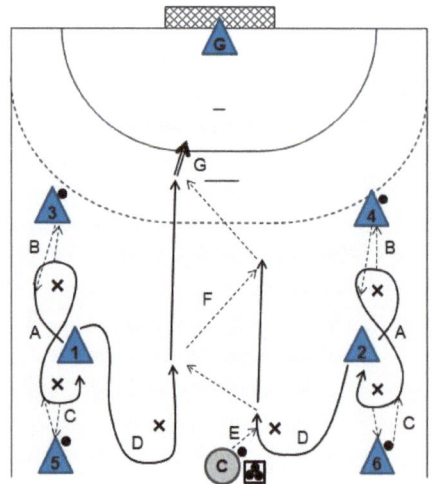

⚠ The players should run the "8 path" smoothly (A). Also, they should not interrupt their running moves when they play and receive a pass.

⚠ On command, the players should run around the cones (D) and keep passing the ball as fast as they can (E, F) until one of them is in shooting position and eventually shoots at the goal (G).

No.: 1-7	Offense/Small groups	10	80

Setting:

- Divide the court in two halves longitudinally with cones.
- Make teams of 2; one team of 2 (3 and 4) should wait at the center line.

Course:

- 1 and 2 try to carry the ball past 1 and to the center line by playing passes (A and D) and moving in a well-coordinated manner (B).
- Each player is allowed to bounce the ball one time (one floor contact) (C).
- As soon as one of the players has stepped on the center line (E), he passes the ball to the group waiting there (F).
- 3 and 4 try to get past 2 by playing passes (G) and moving in a well-coordinated manner (H), and to eventually shoot at the goal (J).
- Afterwards, 5 and 6 start the course over; 1 and 2 stand at the center line, 3 and 4 line up at the goal line.

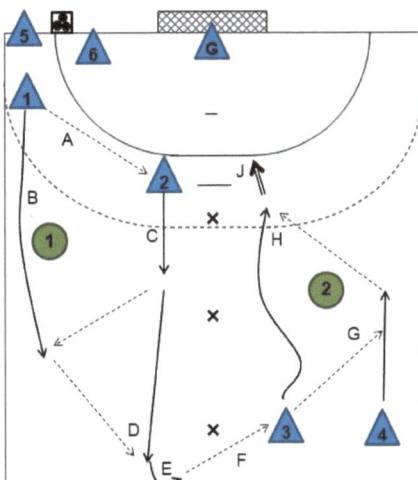

For the defense players:

1. In the beginning, the defense players hold a bib under each arm in order to limit their freedom of movement (the bib must not fall down during the defense actions).
2. Only one bib under one arm.
3. Now the defense players may act without any limitations.

⚠ Switch the defense players at regular intervals.

No.: 1-8	Closing game	10	90

Setting:

- Define a corridor with cones; position a ball box and an empty box as shown in the figure.

Course:

- 1 , 2 , and the goalkeeper play against the remaining players who attack in groups of three.

  The first group of 3 (1 , 2 , and 3) plays 3-on-2 against 1 and 2 . By playing passes (A, B, and D) and breaking away (C), they try to get in shooting position (E).

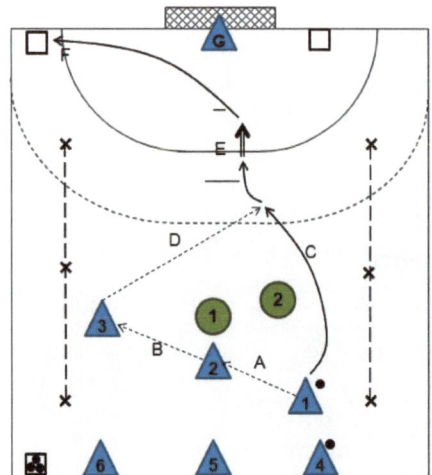

- The attacking players should only dribble the ball if both teammates are being covered by the defense players.
- If the attacking players finish the attack with a goal, they may put the ball into the outmost box (F). If the defense players win the ball, the goalkeeper saves the shot, or the attacking players make a technical mistake, the ball is to be put into the box next to the goal.
- Afterwards, the next group of 3 starts.
- Which team has won most balls, the attacking team or the defending team and the goalkeeper?

⚠ Switch the defense players at regular intervals.

Notes:

_____

_____

_____

_____

_____

_____

No.: 2	Developing and improving the shooting movement		★	90

Opening part		Main part		
X	Warm-up/Stretching		Offense/Individual		Jumping power
	Running exercise		Offense/Small groups	X	Shooting competitions
X	Short game		Offense/Team		Goalkeeper
	Coordination	X	Offense/Series of shots		
	Coordination run		Defense/Individual		**Final part**
	Strengthening		Defense/Small groups		Closing game
X	Ball familiarization		Defense/Team		Final sprint
X	Goalkeeper warm-up shooting		Athletics		
			Endurance		

Key:

✖ Cone

△1 Attacking player

●1 Defense player

▭ Large vaulting box

▣ Ball box

▭ Small vaulting box

● Medicine ball

▱ Large dice

Equipment required:
➔ 12 cones, 6 small vaulting boxes, 2 large vaulting boxes, 4 medicine balls, 2 large foam dices (or small dices), 2 score cards (see below), 2 pens, 2 ball boxes with sufficient number of handballs

Description:
This training unit focuses on acquiring and improving correct shooting movements. This means shooting while standing and shooting while running, without a jump however, in order to highlight arm and body movements. Following a warm-up exercise which already involves shots, the players practice the shoulder and arm rotation for shooting and subsequently combine these moves in a passing competition. In a short game, the players implement the shooting movements in a game situation. This is followed by the goalkeeper warm-up shooting and a closing series of shots which focuses on shooting at the goal.

The training unit consists of the following key exercises:
- Warm-up/Stretching (individual exercise: 15 minutes/total time: 15 minutes)
- Ball familiarization (10/25)
- Ball familiarization (10/35)
- Shooting competitions (15/50)
- Short game (15/65)
- Goalkeeper warm-up shooting (10/75)
- Offense/Series of shots (15/90)

Training unit total time: 90 min.

No.: 2-1	Warm-up/Stretching	15	15

Course 1:

- Each player has a handball. The players crisscross the half of the court while dribbling their ball.
- Once the coach whistles, the players stop, lift their ball over their head with both hands, and vigorously bounce it on the floor so that it flies high up in the air. Afterwards, the players try to catch their ball before it touches the ground.

Course 2:

- The players crisscross the half of the court again. Once the coach whistles, the players run towards the gym wall, bounce their ball against the wall with both hands, and try to catch it (it may bounce on the floor one time).

⚠ Make sure that the players hold their ball over their head in such a way that they do not throw with a hollow back.

Course 3:

- The players crisscross the half of the court again. Once the coach whistles, the players run towards the gym wall, bounce their ball against the wall with their throwing hand, and try to catch it (it may bounce on the floor one time).

Course 4:

- The players crisscross the half of the court again. Once the coach whistles, the players run towards the gym wall, bounce their ball against the wall with their non-throwing hand, and try to catch it (it may bounce on the floor one time).

⚠ Define different targets (basketball board, goalpost, cross bar...) the players should hit.

No.: 2-2	Ball familiarization	10	25

Setting:

- The players make teams of 2. Each team of 2 gets a small vaulting box with a medicine ball on top that serves as the target. Define the shooting distance with two cones.

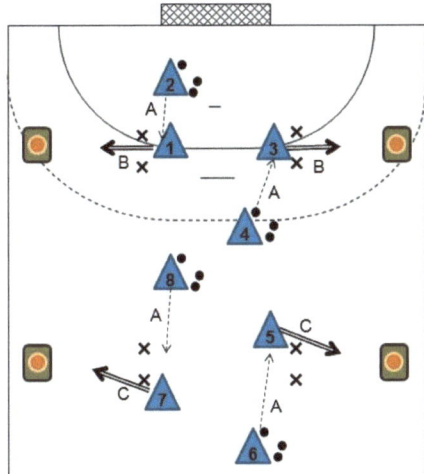

Course 1:

- ▲1 starts as the shooter, ▲2 starts as the feeder.

- ▲2 plays three passes to ▲1 (A).

- ▲1 makes a well-controlled rotation movement and shoots (B).

- While doing this, ▲1 tries to hit the medicine ball.

- Switch tasks after three shots.

- The other groups do the drill in parallel.

- Repeat the drill four times until each player has shot 12 times.

Course 2:

- The basic course remains the same as course 1.

- The shooters shoot three times – from the front center (B), from next to the left cone, and from next to the right cone (C) in order to change the shooting angle and increase the distance.

When the players shoot, observe the following:

⚠ The right-handed player moves forward and plants his left foot firmly on the ground, observing the three-step rule. His toes must point towards the shooting target (figure 1). For left-handed players, the movement is done the other way around.

⚠ The hip and upper body are rotated backwards. The upper arm and elbow must be in line with the shoulder (figure 1).

⚠ The players must keep their elbows up during the passing movement. The hip and upper body are rotated forward with the hip initiating the rotation move (figure 2).

⚠ The players must move the backmost foot forward and rotate the arm forward as well (while keeping the elbow up, however) in order to get a smooth rotation movement (hip, upper body, and arm) (figure 3).

⚠ The backmost foot moves forward, the arm swings forward, and finally the ball is being shot at the target by hinging the wrist (figure 4).

(Figure 1)

(Figure 2)

(Figure 3)

(Figure 4)

| No.: 2-3 | Ball familiarization | 10 | 35 |

Setting:

- Make two teams; each team gets a score card and a pen (see figure).
- For each team, position two medicine balls, two small vaulting boxes, and one large vaulting box as targets. Define the shooting lines using cones (see figure).

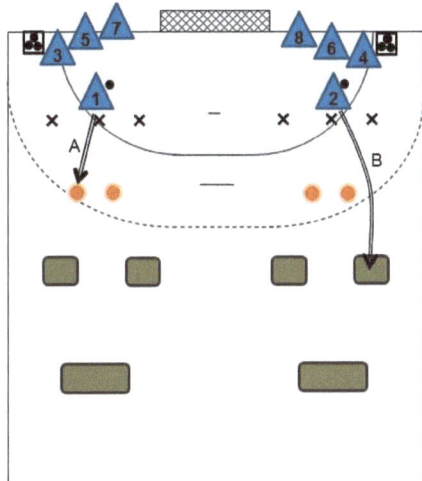

Course:

- 1 and 2 start with a ball and shoot from the shooting line.
- They either try to hit a medicine ball (A), a small vaulting box (B), or the large vaulting box.
- Once they have hit one of the targets, the respective item may be crossed out on the score card (M for medicine ball, B for the small vaulting box, LB for the large vaulting box).
- The player who has shot runs back and exchanges a high-five with the player who is next in line.
- If the team wishes, they may put the medicine balls back into their original position after a hit.
- Which team is first to hit all the targets on the score card (or has scored highest at the end of the playing time)?

Score card: M: medicine ball, B: small vaulting box, LB: large vaulting box

M	M	M	
B	B	B	B
LB	LB	LB	

⚠ Make sure that the players do the shooting movements correctly.

⚠ The players may decide who shoots at which target in order to develop a strategy.

No.: 2-4	Shooting competitions	15	50

Setting:

-   Make two teams. For each team, position three small vaulting boxes and define a shooting line using cones (see figure).
-   Put a medicine ball each on top of the two first boxes, a foam dice each on top of the two second boxes (if no dices are available, use cones or medicine balls), and a cone each on top of the two last boxes.

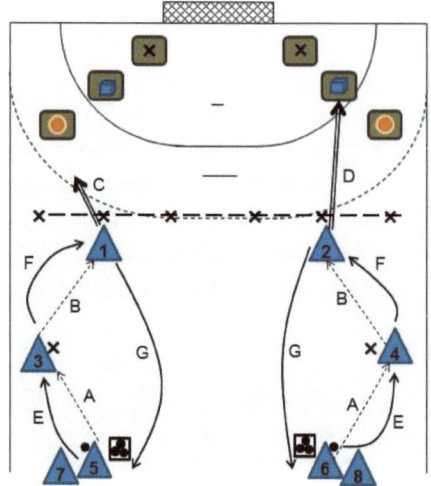

Course:

-   On command, 5 and 6 start and play a pass to 3 and 4 (A).
-   3 and 4 pass the ball to 1 and 2, respectively (B).
-   1 and 2 choose a target and shoot (C and D).
-   When hitting a target, the players receive points as follows:
    o Medicine ball: 2 points
    o Dice: number of points on the dice after it has been hit
    o Cone: 5 points
-   The coach writes down the points of each team. The targets that have been hit must be put back on top of the boxes.
-   After they have played the pass, the players take over the position to which they passed the ball (E and F).
-   7 and 8 each play the next pass.
-   After they have shot, 1 and 2 line up next to the respective ball box (G).
-   Each player must shoot 5 (10) times. The team with the most points wins the game.
-   Consider a second round.

Variant:

-   Limit the playing time. Which team has scored highest after 5 (7) minutes?

⚠ Make sure the players perform the shooting and passing movements correctly.
Revise constantly.

⚠ The players may be given some time before the game in order to develop a
team strategy.

⚠ If there is no foam dice available, the players may shoot at a cone or medicine
ball instead, throw a small dice after a hit, and write down the respective number of
points.

No.: 2-5	Short game	15	65

Setting:

- Define a playing field with cones.
- Make two teams. Label the teams with bibs of different color (in the figure, blue/red plays against green/orange).
- Position three small vaulting boxes with cones or medicine balls on top as targets for each team (see figure).

Course:

- By playing quick passes (A and B) and moving in a well-coordinated manner, the team in ball possession tries to put a player in a good shooting position (C).
- While doing this, the players may pass the ball to a teammate with a bib of another color only (B; pass from red to blue).
- They must not pass the ball to a player with a bib of the same color (D; red to red).
- If the players play a disallowed pass (D), the other team wins the ball.
- If a team has hit a target, the target must not be put back on the box.
- The team which has shot down all the targets on the boxes (or shot down the most targets in the given time) wins.

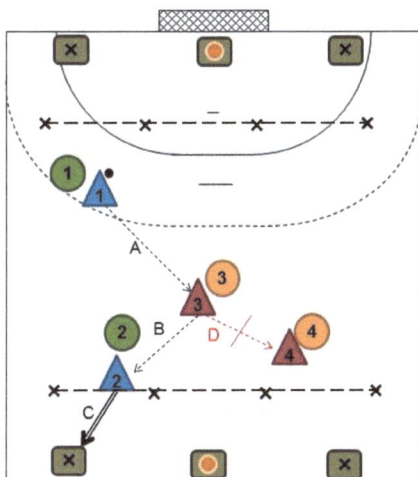

⚠ The players should quickly recognize which teammates are in the ideal
position to receive a pass.

⚠ The players with a bib of different color must run a lot to get into a good
position for a pass.

No.: 2-6	Goalkeeper warm-up shooting	10	75

Setting:
- Define the starting positions with cones (see figure).

Course:

- 5 passes to 3 (A), 3 passes to 1 (B), 1 shoots at the left side of the goal as instructed (hands, top, bottom) (C).

- As soon as 3 passes the ball to 1 (B), 6 passes to 4 (D); then 4 passes to 2 (E), and 2 eventually shoots at the right side of the goal as instructed (F).

- After they have played the pass, the players take over the position to which they passed the ball (G and H).

- The shooting players pick up a new ball from the ball box and line up again (J).

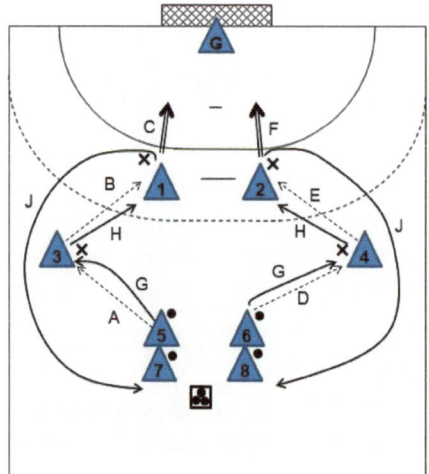

⚠️ The players should time their moves in such a way that there is a series of shots for the goalkeeper.

No.: 2-7	Offense/Series of shots	15	90

Setting:
- Make two teams.
- Define the running paths towards the goal using cones.
- For the second team, define the starting point and the shooting line with cones. Position two small vaulting boxes with foam dices (or medicine balls) on top and a large vaulting box with cones on top (see figure).

Course of team 1:

- 1 starts without a ball and runs a curve around the first cone in the back (A). Once he has run around the cone, he receives the ball from 3 (B), approaches the goal, and shoots (C).

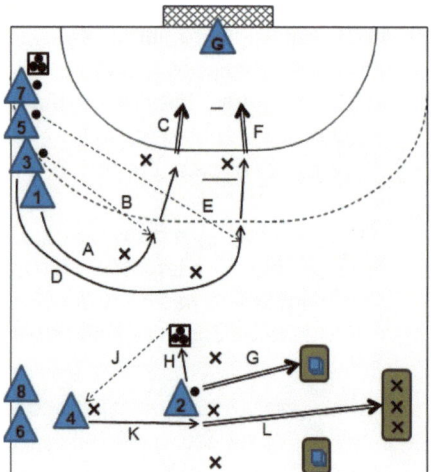

- After the shot, **3** runs around the second cone in the back (D), receives a pass from **5** into his running path (E), and shoots (F).
- Afterwards, **7** starts the same course and receives a pass from **1** (not shown in the figure).
- The players should line up in such a way that they both shoot and pass alternately and run the long and the short way towards the goal alternately.

Course of team 2:

- **2** starts at the shooting line and shoots at one of the targets (G).
- When hitting a target, the players get points as follows:
  - ○ Hitting the dice: The team gets the number of points shown on the dice.
  - ○ Hitting a cone on top of the large vaulting box: The team gets 5 points.
- After his shot, **2** runs to the ball box (H) and passes a ball to **4** (J).
- **4** runs towards the shooting line (K) and shoots (L).
- And so on.

Overall course:

- Team 2 may try to collect points until team 1 has shot 15 goals.
- Switch tasks afterwards.
- Which team has scored highest in the end?

⚠ If there is no foam dice available, the players may shoot at a cone or medicine ball instead, throw a small dice after a hit, and write down the respective number of points.

Notes:

_____

_____

_____

_____

_____

_____

No.: 3	Improving the dribbling technique while observing the game situation		☆	90

Opening part		Main part				
X	Warm-up/Stretching		Offense/Individual			Jumping power
	Running exercise	X	Offense/Small groups	X		Sprint contest
X	Short game		Offense/Team			Goalkeeper
	Coordination	X	Offense/Series of shots			
	Coordination run		Defense/Individual		**Final part**	
	Strengthening		Defense/Small groups	X		Closing game
	Ball familiarization		Defense/Team			Final sprint
X	Goalkeeper warm-up shooting		Athletics			
			Endurance			

Key:

✖ Cone

▲ 1 Attacking player

● 1 Defense player

▣ Ball box

▬ Balance bench

Equipment required:
→ 16 cones of two different colors, 4 balance benches, 4 cards of different color, 4 ball boxes with a sufficient number of handballs

Description:
The objective of this training unit is to improve the dribbling technique focusing on simultaneous observation of the game situation. The players combine movements with dribbling already during the warm-up exercise; in a sprint contest and a short game, they practice dribbling at increased speed. Following the goalkeeper warm-up shooting, there will be a series of shots with additional coordination tasks in which the simultaneous observation of signs will be added. The subsequent small group exercise demands observation of the game situation while dribbling the ball. In a closing game, the players should implement what they practiced before.

The training unit consists of the following key exercises:
- Warm-up/Stretching (individual exercise: 15 minutes/total time: 15 minutes)
- Sprint contest (10/25)
- Short game (15/40)
- Goalkeeper warm-up shooting (10/50)
- Offense/Series of shots (10/60)
- Offense/Small groups (15/75)
- Closing game (15/90)

Training unit total time: 90 min.

No.: 3-1	Warm-up/Stretching	15	15

Setting:
- Make two groups and define a slalom course for each group with cones, as shown in the figure.

Course 1:
- 1 and 1 start and dribble the ball through the slalom course (A). While doing this, they should keep changing the dribbling hand to maintain the greatest possible distance between the cones and the ball.
- After running through the slalom course, 1 and 1 run around the two outmost cones and back again (B). They start over as soon as it is their turn again.
- The next players should start once 1 and 1 have passed the third cone.
- The players each should do the slalom course three times. Change the instructions afterwards.
- Instructions for subsequent rounds:
    o Dribbling through the slalom course while hopping.
    o Dribbling through the slalom course while sidestepping.
    o Dribbling through the slalom course while running backward.

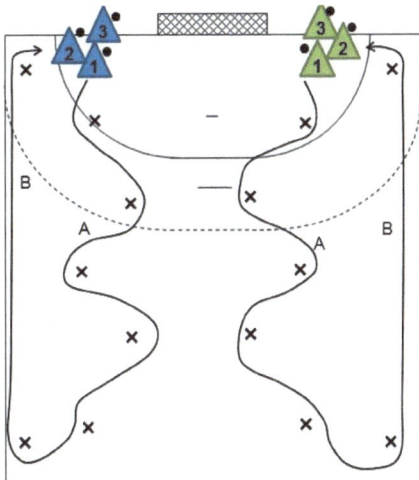

Course 2:
- 1 and 1 start simultaneously on command and dribble the ball through the slalom course (C). While doing this, they should keep changing the dribbling hand to maintain the greatest possible distance between the cones and the ball.
- As soon as the coach whistles, 1 and 1 dribble to the respective other side at once (D) and finish the slalom course on this side (E).

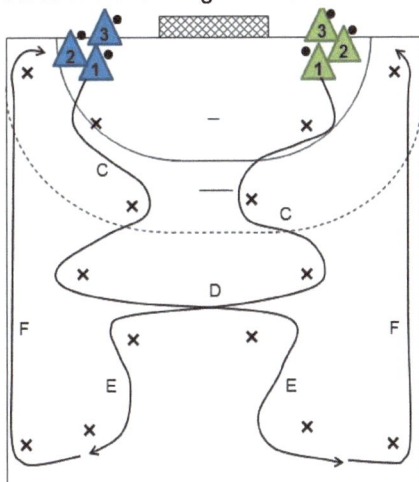

- After running through the slalom course, 🔺 and 🔺 run around the outmost cones and back, and line up again.
- The coach gives the starting sign for the next two players who do the same course.

Afterwards, the players perform stretching/mobilization exercises together.

⚠ Make sure that the players use a proper dribbling technique and change the dribbling hand correctly (no "shoveling"/no holding the ball when changing the direction).

⚠ In course 2, the players should dribble through the course swiftly and change the side quickly once the coach whistles. They should not stop dribbling, however.

No.: 3-2	Sprint contest	10	25

Setting:
- Make two teams and define a slalom course for each team with cones of different color, as shown in the figure.

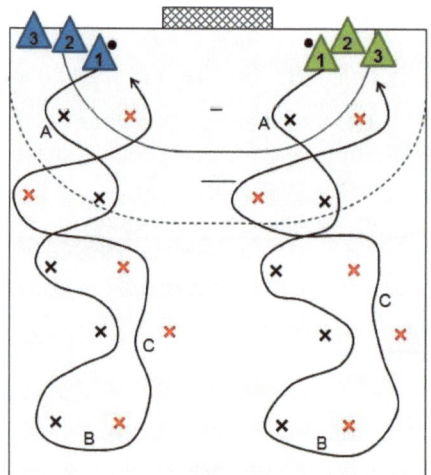

Course 1:

🔺 and 🔺 start simultaneously on command and dribble the ball through the black slalom course (A). While doing this, they should keep changing the dribbling hand to maintain the greatest possible distance between the cones and the ball.

- At the end, the players turn around (B) and run back through the red slalom course (C).
- Afterwards, they hand over the ball to the second player who also runs through both slalom courses, etc.
- Each player does the course twice. The team which has run through the course fastest gets a point.
- Which team has scored highest after three rounds?

Course 2:

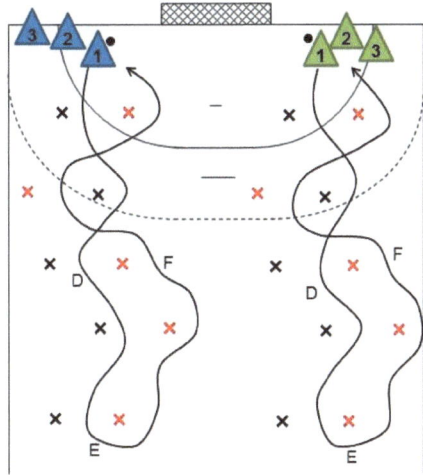

- ▲ and ▲ start simultaneously on command and dribble the ball. Now, they have to run through the course in such a way that the black cones are next to the right hand of the player (D), i.e. the players should dribble with their left hand.
- At the end, the players turn around (E) and run back through the course in such a way that the red cones are next to the left hand of the player (F), i.e. the players dribble with their right hand.
- Afterwards, they hand over the ball to the second player who also runs through the course while observing the same rules, etc.
- Each player does the course twice. The team which has run through the course fastest gets a point.
- Which team has scored highest after three rounds?

No.: 3-3	Short game	15	40

Setting:

- Use four balance benches to divide the playing field into four quarters.
- Make four teams and assign one ball box (same number of handballs) and one quarter to each team.
- The coach has three colored cards. Each color is assigned to a running direction (right, left, diagonal).

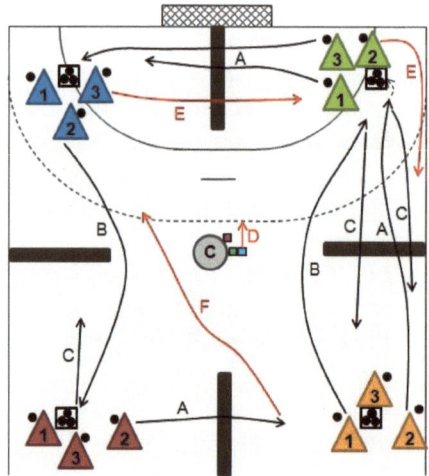

Course:

- Once the coach whistles, the players of each team start to pick up the balls from their box and to put them into the other teams' boxes (A).
- The card which the coach shows defines the running direction (in the example, the coach shows the red card, i.e. the players must put the balls into the box of their neighbors on the right).
- The players may decide themselves whether to dribble over the bench (A) or to run around it (B).
- As soon as a ball has been put into the respective target box, the players jump over the bench, return to their own ball box (C) and pick up a new ball.
- The coach may change the color during the game (in the example, the coach shows a blue card instead of a red one (D)).
- The players change the direction as fast as they can and now put the balls into the box of their neighbors on the left (E).
- Players who have already left their own quarter may take a shortcut (F).
- As soon as the coach shows the third color (green in the example), the players run to the diagonal box. Now the players do not have to jump over the benches, but now must take care of "oncoming traffic".
- After about 3 to 4 minutes, the players count the balls. The team with the fewest balls in their box wins the game and gets a point. The team with the most balls in their box gets a penalty point.
- Which team has scored highest after three (four) rounds?

⚠ While dribbling – before putting the ball into the box at the latest – the players should look to the coach and check whether the playing direction has changed and whether they still approach the correct ball box.

⚠ The coach must make sure that the players put the balls into the correct box.

| No.: 3-4 | Goalkeeper warm-up shooting | 10 | 50 |

Setting:

- Position ball boxes, cones, and balance benches as shown in the figure.

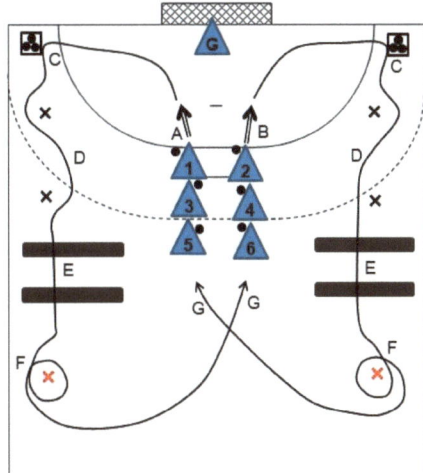

Course:

- **1** shoots at the left side of the goal as instructed (hands, top, middle, bottom) (A); a bit delayed,

  2 shoots at the right side of the goal as instructed (B), etc., in such a way that the goalkeeper faces a series of shots.
- After the shot, the players run to the ball box, pick up a new ball (C), run around the black cones in slalom (D), run over the bench as instructed (E), run around the red cone completely (F), and line up on the other side (G).

Instructions for running over the benches:

- Step onto the bench with one foot and bounce the ball on the bench one time.
- Step onto the bench with one foot and bounce the ball on the floor only.
- Bounce the ball on the bench one time and climb/jump over the bench with both feet.
- Jump over the bench; neither the feet nor the ball must touch the bench.

⚠ Make sure the players use a proper dribbling technique; they should increase their speed only gradually. The players should not hold the ball, if possible, but rather dribble it all the time.

No.: 3-5	Offense/Series of shots	10	60

Setting:

- The coach stands behind/next to the goal and has four colored cards. Each corner of the goal is assigned a color.

Course 1:

- **2** stands face to face with **1**, with his back turned to the goal.

- **1** bounces the ball next to **2** so that it further bounces in direction of the goal (A).

- **2** turns around, runs after the ball, and tries to further dribble the ball (without taking it up with both hands) (B, C).

- **2** shoots at the goal (D).

- Afterwards, the next teams of 2 do the same course. They change tasks in the second round.

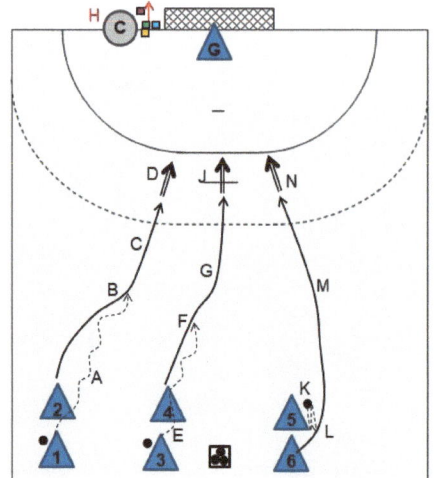

Course 2:

- **4** stands in front of **3**, his face turned to the goal.

- **3** dribbles the ball through the legs of **4** (E), **4** runs after the ball, further dribbles it without taking it up with both hands (F), and keeps dribbling towards the goal (G).

- While the players dribble towards the goal (G), the coach shows a colored card (H); **4** must shoot at the respective corner (J).

- Afterwards, the next teams of 2 do the same course. They change tasks in the second round.

Course 3:

- **5** stands in front of **6** with his face turned towards **6**, and dribbles a ball (K).

- **6** steals the ball (L) and then dribbles towards the goal (M).

- While the players dribble towards the goal (M), the coach shows a colored card (H); **6** must shoot at the respective corner (N).

- Afterwards, the next teams of 2 do the same course. They change tasks in the second round.

⚠️ The players should look to the coach while dribbling in order to quickly recognize the color and the target corner; they should not slow down, however.

No.: 3-6	Offense/Small groups	15	75

Setting:

- Position cones as shown in the figure.

Course 1 (figure 1):

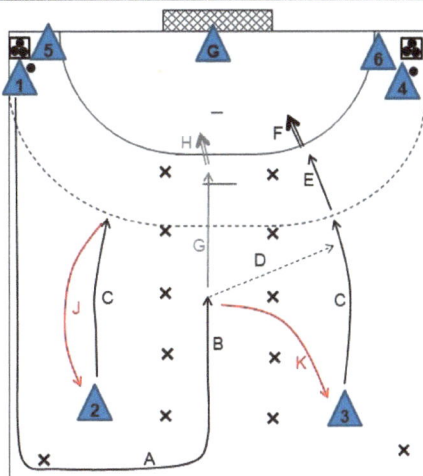

- 1 starts with a ball, dribbles around the backmost cone (A) and into the lane of cones (B).
- As soon as he has entered the lane, 2 and 3 start at the backmost cone of the lane and run along with 1, a few meters in front of him (C).
- At any point in time, one of the two players (2 or 3) lifts a hand.
- 1 passes the ball (D) to this player as fast as he can (3 in the figure). 3 dribbles towards the goal (E) and shoots (F).
- If none of the players lifts a hand, 1 dribbles to the 6-meter zone (G) and shoots himself (H); if both players lift a hand, 1 decides who will receive the pass.
- 3 lines up at the wing position after the shot, 2 moves back to his initial position (J), 1 takes over the vacant position (K).
- Afterwards, 4 starts the course on the other side.

Course 2 (figure 2):

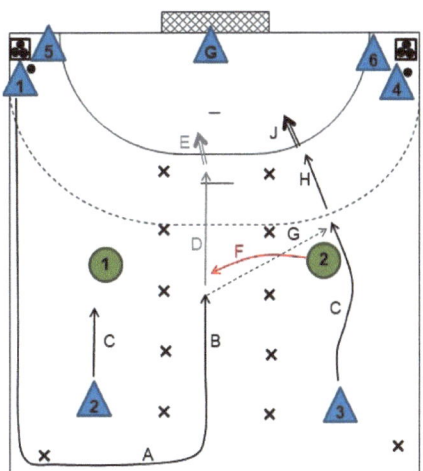

- 1 and 2 are the defense players, standing in their initial position in front of 2 and 3.
- The basic course remains the same (A, B, and C); however, 2 and 3 do not lift a hand as a sign anymore, but 1 should rather react according to the defense players' behavior.
- If none of the defense players enters the corridor, 1 dribbles to the 6-meter line (D) and shoots (E).

- If one of the defense players makes a step towards ▲ (F), ▲ passes the ball to the uncovered teammate (G) who eventually shoots at the goal (H and J).

⚠ The players should analyze the situation while dribbling and react and pass the ball accordingly, either on the basis of a hand sign or the defense players' behavior.

⚠ Switch the defense players at regular intervals in course 2.

No.: 3-7	Closing game	15	90

Setting:
- Position cones as shown in the figure.
- Make two teams.

Course:

- ▲ starts with a ball, dribbles around the backmost cone (A) and through the two cones in the center (B).

- From that moment, ▲, ▲, and ▲ play a free 3-on-2 game against ● and ● (C, D, and E) until one of them has shot at the goal or the defense players have won the ball.

- Following the attack, the two players of the blue team who did not shoot (or lose the ball) become the defense players; the shooting player (third attacking player) lines up behind ▲.

- ● and ● run to the backmost cones and start the next attack for the green team, together with ● who dribbles around the backmost cone (F) and through the cones in the center in order to initiate the attack.

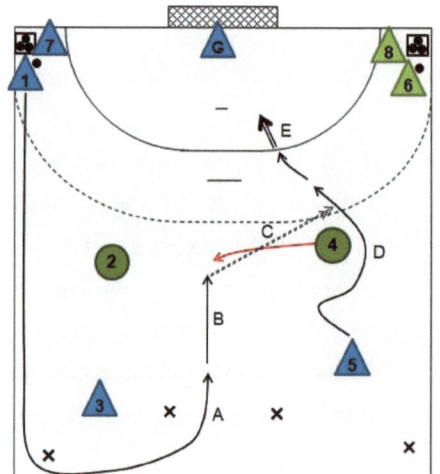

- Subsequently, 2, 4, and 6 play a free 3-on-2 game until one of them has shot at the goal or the defense players have won the ball (G to L).
- Which team has shot the most goals?

⚠ If the defense players win the ball, they pass it to the goalkeeper who again passes it to the players waiting in line. An attack is started by the attacking player on the wing position (dribbling).

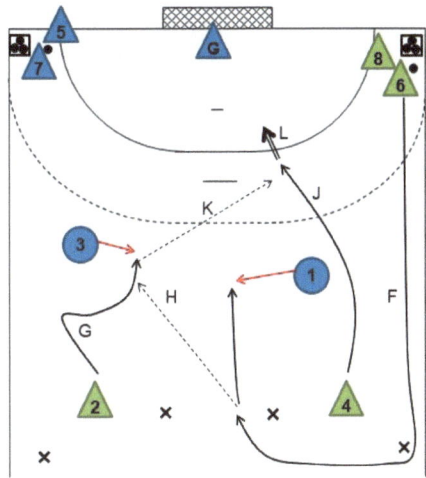

Notes:

_____

_____

_____

_____

_____

_____

_____

_____

No.: 4	Breaking away from man coverage using running feints	⭐	90

Opening part		Main part				
X	Warm-up/Stretching	X	Offense/Individual		Jumping power	
	Running exercise	X	Offense/Small groups	X	Sprint contest	
X	Short game		Offense/Team		Goalkeeper	
	Coordination		Offense/Series of shots			
	Coordination run		Defense/Individual		**Final part**	
	Strengthening		Defense/Small groups	X	Closing game	
	Ball familiarization		Defense/Team		Final sprint	
X	Goalkeeper warm-up shooting		Athletics			
			Endurance			

Key:

✖   Cone

🔺1   Attacking player

🟢1   Defense player

◼   Ball box

Equipment required:

➔ 16 cones, 1 ball box with sufficient number of handballs, DIN A4 posters with drawn symbols

Description:

This training unit focuses on breaking away from man coverage without a ball, by means of running feints. Following warm-up, a sprint contest with changes of direction, and a team ball variant, the players practice quick changes of direction one more time during the goalkeeper warm-up shooting exercise. Subsequently, there will be an individual offense exercise focusing on breaking away by means of running feints. The players will further elaborate this topic in two small group exercises and finally implement what they practiced before in free play.

The training unit consists of the following key exercises:
- Warm-up/Stretching (individual exercise: 10 minutes/total time: 10 minutes)
- Sprint contest (10/20)
- Short game (10/30)
- Goalkeeper warm-up shooting (10/40)
- Offense/Individual (15/55)
- Offense/Small groups (10/65)
- Offense/Small groups (15/80)
- Closing game (10/90)

Training unit total time: 90 min.

No.: 4-1	Warm-up/Stretching	10	10

Course:
- Each player has a handball.
- The coach specifies different exercises which the players do within the 9-meter zone (dribbling with the throwing/non-throwing hand; dribbling with both hands alternately; dribbling through the legs; dribble, sit down and get up).
- After 1-2 minutes, the coach shows a DIN A4 poster with a symbol drawn on it (a circle, a square, a rectangle, a sinuous line, a zigzag line as in the letter "Z", two parallel lines, etc.).
- As soon as the players have recognized the symbol on the poster, they should create this symbol together with their bodies lying on the floor. However, they must dribble all the time.
- If the players managed to reconstruct the symbol, they start the next exercise within the 9-meter zone, as instructed.

No.: 4-2	Sprint contest	10	20

Setting:
- Make two teams.
- Position 5-6 cones per team on the floor, a bit offset to each other.

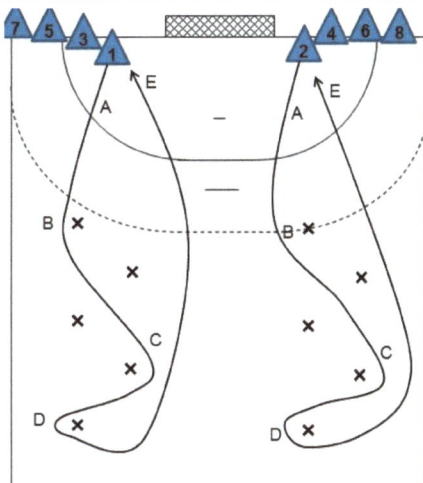

Course:
- The cones are assigned the numbers 1 to 5.
- The coach calls out three numbers (e.g. 1-4-5) as starting sign for **1** and **2**.
- **1** and **2** sprint to the cones (A), around the three specified cones (B, C, and D), and touch each one with the hand that is closer to the cones (1 (B) and 5 (D) with the left hand, 4 (C) with the right hand).
- Afterwards, **1** and **2** sprint back and exchange a high five with the next player (E).
- The player who first exchanges the high five gets a point for his team.
- Now the coach gives the next sign, and **3** and **4** start the course.
- And so on.

⚠ When calling out the numbers, make sure that the players have to change the direction several times, if possible (even and uneven numbers alternately).

No.: 4-3	Short game	10	30

Setting:

- Divide the playing field into two fields using cones (see figure).

Course:

- Two teams play team ball in one of the two playing fields.
- While doing this, the team in ball possession tries to play 10 passes in a row (A-D), avoiding that the other team wins the ball.
  If the coach whistles one time, the ball must be passed into the other field (F). In order to do this, the players move to the other field (E).
- Afterwards, they keep playing on this field. If the coach whistles one more time, the players change the playing field again, etc.
- If a team has managed to pass the ball 10 times in a row, the other team must do a short extra task (jumping jacks, push-ups, jumps, or similar).
- Then the teams start over with the former defending team in ball possession.

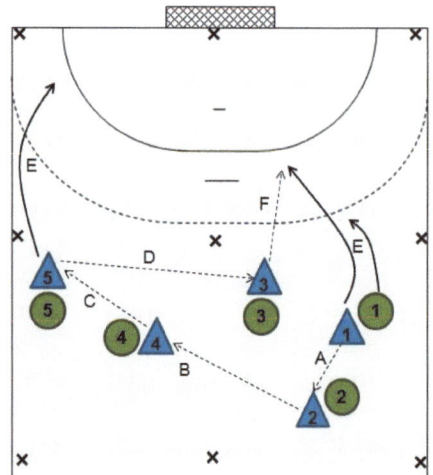

⚠ The defense players should maintain a close man coverage; the attacking players should move in a well-coordinated manner in order to play 10 passes in a row.

⚠ Once the coach whistles, the attacking and defending players should react at once and move to the other field immediately.

No.: 4-4	Goalkeeper warm-up shooting	10	40

Setting:

- Position cone goals on both sides of the field, a bit offset to each other and at a varying distance.

Course:

- **1** starts approaching the goal with a ball (A) and shoots at the left side of the goal as instructed (hands, top, bottom) (B).

- **2** starts a bit delayed (C) and shoots at the right side of the goal as instructed (D).

- After the shot, **1** runs to the left and through the cone goals as fast as he can (E), swiftly changing directions (F).

- **2** runs to the right after the shot (G) and sprints through the cone goals on the right side.

- The players line up on the other side with a new ball so that the goalkeeper faces a long series of shots.

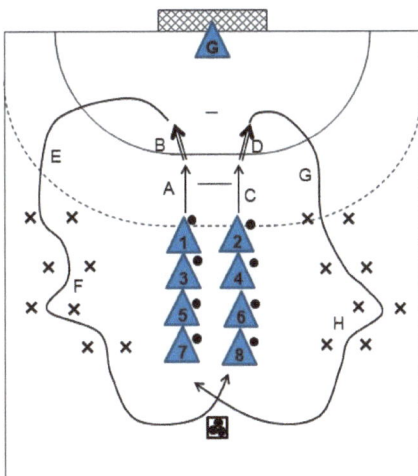

⚠ The players should time their shots in such a way that there is a series for the goalkeeper.

⚠ The players should sprint through the cones as fast as they can.

No.: 4-5	Offense/Individual	15	55

Setting:

- Define a corridor with cones and divide it into two zones.

Course:

- **1** passes to **2** (A), enters the first zone, and tries to get past **1** by means of running feints (B).

- As soon as **1** is in the position to receive a pass, **2** passes the ball back to **1** (C) and keeps on running towards the goal (D).

- Before entering the second zone, **1** passes the ball to **2** one more time (E) and then tries to get past **2** by means of running feints again (F).

- As soon as **1** has left the second zone and approaches the goal, **2** passes him the ball (G), and **1** shoots at the goal (H).

- Afterwards, **3** and **4** start the same course.

- **2** lines up in the center with a ball, **1** becomes the feeder/receiver.

- The players should run along on the left and right side of the corridor alternately.

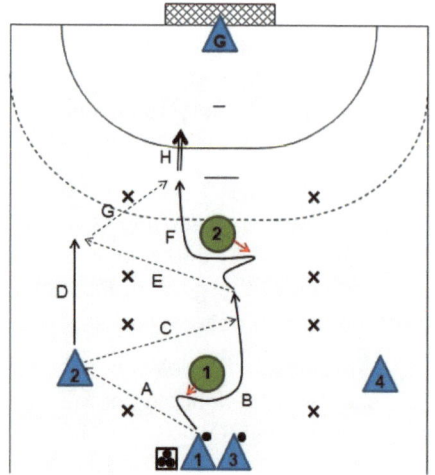

⚠ After playing the pass to the feeder/receiver, the players should try to lure the defending player into a certain direction with a running feint, and then quickly cross the zone.

⚠ The feeders/receivers should run along and get into an ideal passing position over and over.

No.: 4-6	Offense/Small groups	10	65

Setting:

- Position a cone goal about 1 meter in front of the center line and another cone right in front of the cone goal. Define the shooting zones for the back position players at the 7-meter line with two cones (see figure).

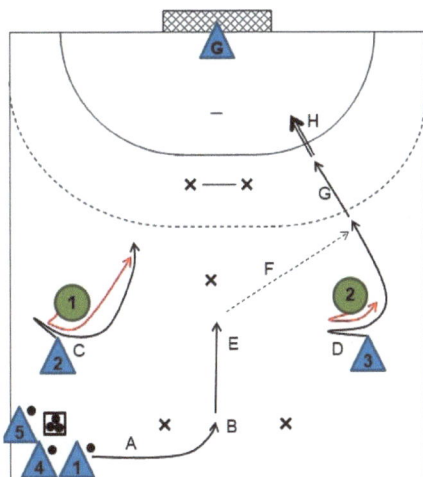

Course:

- **1** starts to dribble (A) and runs through the cone goal at the center line (B).

- As soon as **1** has arrived at the cone goal, **2** and **3** may try to break away from the man coverage by **1** and **2** (C and D) and get into an ideal passing position. While doing this, **2** and **3** must stay in their corridor of cones.

- **1** keeps dribbling towards the cone in the center (E).

- Once a player has managed to break away, **1** takes up the ball and passes it to his uncovered teammate (F) (**3** in the example).

- **3** approaches the goal (G) and shoots (H).

- As soon as **1** has arrived at the cone, he must take up the ball. **2** and **3** must get into a good passing position within 3 seconds at the latest.

- The player who shot at the goal (**3** in the example) lines up behind **5** with a new ball while **1** takes over his previous position.

⚠ **1** should observe his teammates already when dribbling towards the cone (E) so that he can pass the ball immediately once **2** or **3** have managed to break away.

⚠ **2** and **3** should use running feints, find the right timing, and get into a good passing position for **1**.

⚠ Switch the defense players at regular intervals.

No.: 4-7	Offense/Small groups	15	80

Setting:

-   Position a cone goal about 1 meter in front of the center line.

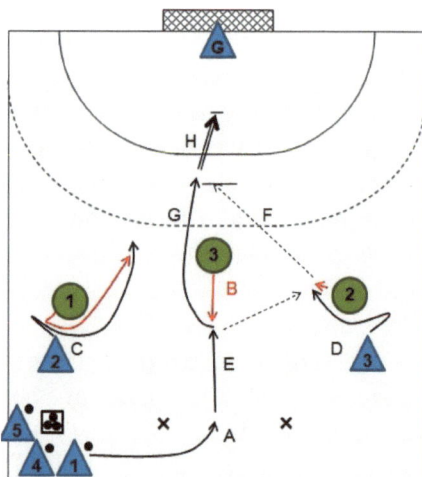

Course:

-   **1** starts to dribble and runs through the cone goal at the center line (A).

-   **3** initially starts at the 9-meter line. As soon as **1** has arrived the cone goal, **3** may step forward towards him (B).

-   **1**, **2**, and **3** now play a free 3-on-3 game trying to overcome the offensive man coverage by **1**, **2** and **3** until they have shot at the goal (H) or the defense players have won the ball.

-   **1** tries to approach the goal (E) until **3** forces him to take up the ball or until **2** or **3** have managed to break away (C and D).

-   **1** passes the ball to the uncovered teammate and then tries to break away and get into a good passing position himself (G).

-   In case of a shot at the goal, the shooting player lines up again behind **5** with a ball, the other two players go back to their initial positions next to **1** and **2**, and **4** starts the course over.

-   If there is no shot at the goal, the attacking player who was last in ball possession lines up behind **5**.

⚠ The player in ball possession must observe his teammates so that he can pass the ball immediately after one of his teammates has managed to break free and gained positional advantage towards the goal.

⚠ The players who are not in ball possession should use running feints to get past the defense players.

⚠ Switch the defense players at regular intervals.

| No.: 4-8 | Closing game | 10 | 90 |

Setting:

- Make two teams. Both teams play 3-on-3 against each other on each half of the playing field.
- The center line divides the playing field; the six players each stay in their half. The players must not cross the center line (A).

Course:

- The attacking players should try to get into a good passing position (C) by breaking away over and over (B).
- After a goal, the goalkeeper takes the throw-off (D).

- Switch the playing fields after a couple of minutes.

Variants:

- Limit the number of passes to be played in each half of the playing field.

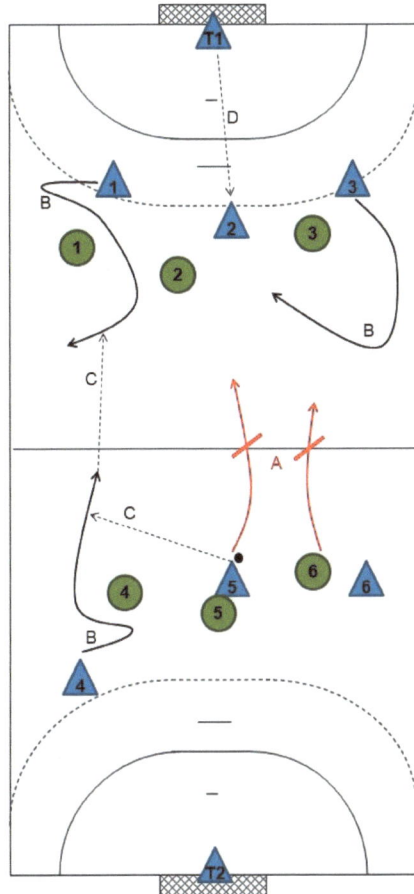

Notes:

No.: 5	Gaining positional advantage using passing feints		☆	90

Opening part		Main part				
X	Warm-up/Stretching	X	Offense/Individual		Jumping power	
	Running exercise	X	Offense/Small groups		Sprint contest	
X	Short game		Offense/Team		Goalkeeper	
	Coordination	X	Offense/Series of shots			
	Coordination run		Defense/Individual		**Final part**	
	Strengthening		Defense/Small groups	X	Closing game	
X	Ball familiarization		Defense/Team		Final sprint	
X	Goalkeeper warm-up shooting		Athletics			
			Endurance			

Key:

✗   Cone

△1   Attacking player

●1   Defense player

▣   Ball box

⊥   Pole

Equipment required:

➔ 12 cones (of different color), 2 poles, 2 ball boxes with sufficient number of handballs

Description:

The key topics of this training unit are passing feints and how to combine them with a breakthrough or a return pass to a teammate. Following a warm-up running exercise, the players already learn how to pass the ball cleverly in a short game; this will be further developed in the ball familiarization phase. In the goalkeeper warm-up shooting exercise, the players practice passing feints in combination with a 1-on-1 breakthrough; in the subsequent series of shots, they combine the passing feint with a return pass to their teammate. Both variants will be implemented twice in the subsequent 1-on-1, 3-on-2, and 4-on-4 games.

The training unit consists of the following key exercises:

- Warm-up/Stretching (individual exercise: 10 minutes/total time: 10 minutes)
- Short game (10/20)
- Ball familiarization (15/35)
- Goalkeeper warm-up shooting (10/45)
- Offense/Series of shots (10/55)
- Offense/Individual (10/65)
- Offense/Small groups (15/80)
- Closing game (10/90)

Training unit total time: 90 min.

No.: 5-1	Warm-up/Stretching	10	10

Setting:

- Position cones of different color outside of the 9-meter zone.

Course:

- Each player has a handball. The players do different exercises with a ball within the 9-meter zone (see below).
- At any point in time, the coach calls out a color (e.g. "blue").
- This is the sign for the players to dribble around one of the blue cones and then move back into the 9-meter zone.
- The last players must do a short extra task (e.g. jumping jacks, sit-ups, or similar).

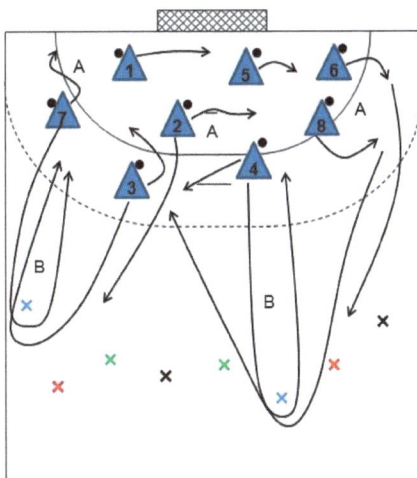

Exercises in the 9-meter zone:

- Dribbling with the left/right hand alternately.
- Hopping and dribbling simultaneously.
- Throwing the ball in the air and catch it.
- Hand over the ball through the legs from one side to the other alternately.

Extension:

- Assign words to the individual cones (apple, pear, plum, banana) and call out one of these words instead of a color.

No.: 5-2	Short game	10	20

Setting:

- Use cones to define corridors (3 to 5, depending on the number of players).
- In each corridor, there are 2 defending players and three attacking players alternately (two attacking players are sufficient in the first corridor).

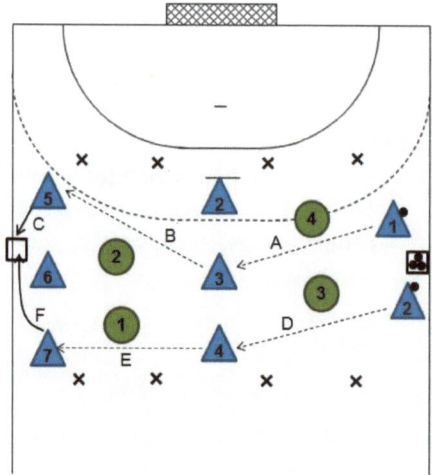

Course:

- The attacking players must pass all the balls from the ball box from one side to the other side and put them into the box as fast as they can.

- 1 passes the first ball to an attacking player in the third corridor (A) who passes the ball to the final corridor (B) where the players finally lay the ball into the box (C).

- 2 starts the same course a bit delayed (D, E, and F).

- Once he has played the pass, 1 picks up a new ball etc.

- The defense players should try to block the balls or to steal them while moving inside their corridor. If they succeed, they must pass the ball back to 1 or 2 immediately.

- Stop the time as soon as all the balls are in the target box. Afterwards, repeat the exercise with four new defending players and switch the tasks of the attacking players.

- Which defending team is able to block the attacking players for the longest time?

⚠ The players should quickly identify which attacking player in the next corridor is in the best position to receive a pass.

⚠ Maybe give the hint to feint a pass (so that the defending players run to the respective attacking player) and then pass to the free player.

No.: 5-3	Ball familiarization	15	35

Setting:

- Make groups of 4 and define a playing field with cones for each group (or use existing lines on the gym floor to define the fields).

Course:

- The four players go into their field.
- ▲1, ▲2, and ▲3 try to pass the ball 10 times in a row (A and B), without ⬤1 touching the ball or the player in ball possession. While doing this, the players are not allowed to leave the field.
- If ▲1, ▲2, and ▲3 have managed to pass the ball 10 times in a row or if ⬤1 has won the ball, another player becomes the new defense player.
- The other groups do the course in parallel in other fields (C).

⚠ The attacking players should quickly identify which teammate is in the position to receive a pass. Maybe give the hint to feint a pass (so that the defending players run to the respective attacking player) and then pass to the free player.

No.: 5-4	Goalkeeper warm-up shooting	10	45

Setting:

- Position a pole as marking sign.

Course:

- 2 passes the ball to 1 (A), starts to run, and receives a return pass (B).

- Afterwards, 2 makes a passing feint (C) to the right (vigorous and well-controlled rotation movement, viewing direction to the right), runs to the left and past the pole (D), and eventually shoots at the goal as instructed (hands, top, bottom) (E).

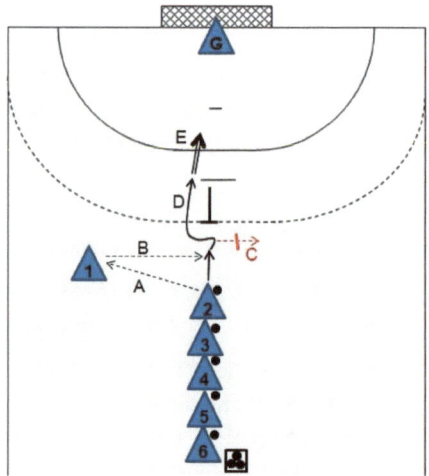

- Once 2 has finished his running feint, 3 starts the same course.

- Change 1 in the next round.

⚠ The players should make an authentic passing feint to the right (vigorous shoulder rotation and well-controlled trunk rotation movement to the side) before taking a turn and approaching the goal.

⚠ Change the side of the passing feint after each round.

⚠ For right-handed players, a passing feint to the right is easier. When the players make a passing feint to the left, make sure they use a proper technique. Vice-versa for left-handed players.

No.: 5-5	Offense/Series of shots	10	55

Setting:

- Position two poles as marking signs.

Course:

- **2** passes the ball to **1** (A), does a piston movement (B), and receives a return pass (C).

- Afterwards, **2** makes a passing feint towards **3** (E) and passes the ball back to **1** who runs past the pole on the inner side, after making a running feint (D).

- **1** shoots (F).

- Subsequently, the players start the course on the other side, with **4** and **3**.

- **1** lines up for the center back position after the shot, **2** moves to the left back position after the action.

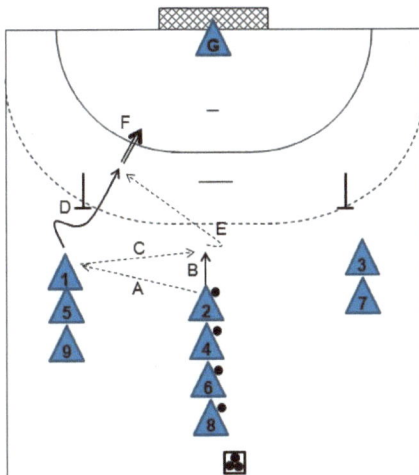

⚠ The players should make an authentic passing feint (vigorous shoulder rotation and well-controlled trunk rotation movement to the side) before passing the ball to the other side.

No.: 5-6	Offense/Individual	10	65

Setting:

- Define two corridors using cones (see figure).

Course:

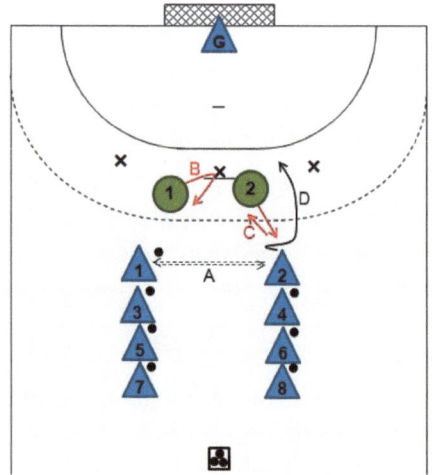

- 🔺1 and 🔺2 pass a ball (A).

- The defense players 🟢1 and 🟢2 step forward towards the player in ball possession and – once he passed the ball – touch the cone in the center (B) before stepping forward again.

- 🔺1 and 🔺2 use passing feints in order to break through themselves on the outer side (D), if the defense player has moved away too soon (C).

- Afterwards, 🔺3 and 🔺4 start the same course.

- Switch the defense players at regular intervals.

⚠️ The players should make authentic passing feints and hence force the defense players to leave their defense position too soon so that they can break through.

No.: 5-7	Offense/Small groups	15	80

Setting:

- Define the playing field with cones.

Course:

- 1, 2, and 3 play 3-on-2 against 1 and 2.
- The players must not cross nor play with a second pivot, but rather play the following variants:
  - o The players on the back positions keep passing the ball (A and B).
  - o One player (2) does a vigorous piston movement as if he was about to approach the goal (C).
  - o Afterwards, 2 feints a pass to 1 (D), fools the defense players, and passes the ball to 3 who also does a piston movement (E). If the defense players have been fooled, 3 shoots at the goal (F).
  - o One player (1) does a vigorous piston movement as if he was about to approach the goal (G).
  - o Afterwards, 1 feints a pass to 2 and tries to fool the defense players in order to break through on the outer side himself (H).
- After the action, the next group of 3 starts.
- Switch the defense players at regular intervals.

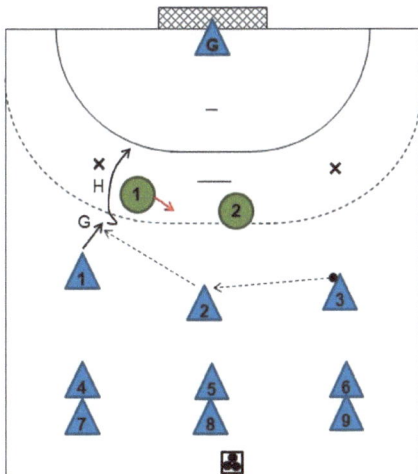

⚠ The players should make authentic passing feints and hence force the defense players to leave their position too soon so that they can break through or play a return pass.

No.: 5-8	Closing game	15	90

Setting:
- Define the playing field with cones as shown in the figure (adjust to the players' level of performance).

Course:
- ① initially plays 1-on-4 against ▲1, ▲2, ▲3, and ▲4.
- For each goal the attacking player have shot, another defense player may enter the playing field (A).
- As soon as all four defense players have entered the game, the attacking players may use the whole width of the playing field to score goals.
- How many attacks are necessary until the attacking players have scored a goal 4-on-4? Afterwards, the teams switch tasks.
- Which team needs fewer attacks?

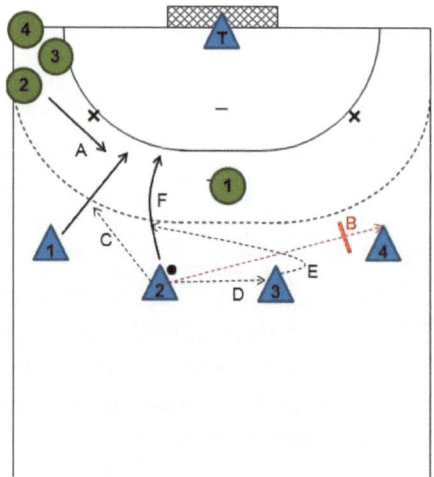

Rules for the attacking players:
- The ball must be passed from one position to the next only; the players must not skip any positions.
- The players must keep their positions; they must not play with a second pivot nor make crossing moves.
- When passing, the players must not skip any positions (B).
- The attacking players may either:
    o Break through immediately after receiving a pass (A)
    o Or use passing feints (D, E, and F).

Notes:

_____

_____

_____

_____

_____

5. About the editor

JÖRG MADINGER, born in Heidelberg (Germany) in 1970

July 2014 (further training): 3-day coaching workshop: "Basic components of goalkeeper training", held by the **German Handball Association (Deutscher Handballbund, DHB)**
Lecturers: Michael Neuhaus, Renate Schubert, Marco Stange, Norbert Potthoff, Olaf Gritz, Andreas Thiel, Henning Fritz

May 2014 (further training): 3-day coaching further training during the VELUX EHF Final4, held by the **German Handball Coaching Association (Deutsche Handball Trainer Vereinigung, DHTV)/DHB**
Lecturers: Jochen Beppler (DHB coach), Christian vom Dorff (DHB referee), Mark Dragunski (coach of TuSeM Essen, Germany), Klaus-Dieter Petersen (DHB coach), Manolo Cadenas (coach of the Spanish national team)

May 2013 (further training): 3-day coaching further training during the VELUX EHF Final4, held by the **DHTV/DHB**
Lecturers: Prof. Dr. Carmen Borggrefe (University of Stuttgart, Germany), Klaus-Dieter Petersen (DHB coach), Dr. Georg Froese (sports psychologist), Jochen Beppler (DHB base camp coach), Carsten Alisch (young talents' hockey coach)

Since July 2012: A-License, DHB

Since February 2011: Handball club trainings, coaching (training and competitive areas)

November 2011: Foundation of the Handball Specialist Publishing Company (Handball Fachverlag) (handall-uebungen.de, Handball Practice and Special Handball Practice)

May 2009: Foundation of the handball online platform handball-uebungen.de

2008-2010: Youth coordinator and youth coach, SG Leutershausen (Germany)

Since 2006: B-License

Editor's note
In 1995, a friend convinced me to join him in coaching a handball youth team (male, under 13 years of age).

This was the beginning of my career as a team handball coach. Ever since I enjoyed working as a coach and had high requirements concerning my exercises. Soon, the standard pool of exercises wasn't enough for me anymore and I started to modify and develop drills myself.

Today, I coach a broad range of youth and adult teams with different performance levels and adjust my training units to the individual needs of the teams.

A few years ago, I started selling my exercises and drills online at handball-uebungen.de. Since, in handball training, there is a tendency towards a general athletic training that focuses on coordination work – especially in the training of youth teams –, a large number of my games and exercises can be applied to other sports as well.

Get inspired by the various game concepts, be creative, and rely on your own experiences!

Yours sincerely,
Jörg Madinger

6. Further reference books published by DV Concept

From warm-up to handball team play – 75 exercises for every handball training unit

By making your training units more diverse, you can increase the players' motivation, since you consistently offer new approaches to improve and refine familiar movement sequences. In this book, you will find inspiring exercises you can apply during each phase of your everyday team handball training – from warm-up and goalkeeper warm-up shooting to the common contents of the main phase and the closing games. Each exercise is illustrated and described in an easy, comprehensible manner. Specific notes give you tips on what you need to be aware of.

This book deals with the following key subjects:

Warm-up:
- Basic warm-up
- Short warm-up games
- Sprint contests
- Coordination
- Ball familiarization
- Goalkeeper warm-up shooting

Basic exercises, basic play, and target play:
- Offense/series of shots
- General offense
- Fast throw-off
- 1st and 2nd wave
- Defensive action
- Closing games
- Endurance

At the end of this book, you will find an entire methodological training unit. The objective of this training unit is to improve shooting and quick decision-making under pressure.

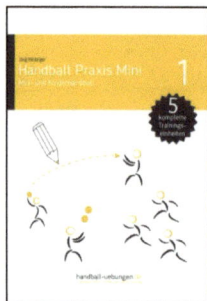

Minihandball training and handball training for young kids (5 training units)

Minihandball training and handball training for kids is different from handball training for older players and considerably different from handball training for competitive players. During their first contact with "handball", kids should be familiarized with the ball in a playful way. They should be taught that being active, doing sports, playing together, and even playing against each other is fun.

This book contains a short introduction to handball for kids and young children and its special characteristics as well as example exercises which help to make your training units interesting and more diverse.

Following this, there are five complete training units of different difficulty levels that focus on the basic handball techniques (dribbling, passing, catching, shooting, and defending in a game with opponents). The kids are playfully introduced to the subsequent handball-specific basics. At the same time, particular attention is payed to general physical experience and the development of coordination skills.

The exercises are illustrated and described in an easy, comprehensible manner. They can be immediately integrated in every training unit. By using the given training variants, you can easily adjust the difficulty level of the training units to the respective target group. The variants should also encourage you to modify and further develop the exercises to make each training unit a new and more diverse experience for the children.

Passing and catching while moving – 60 exercises for each handball training unit

Passing and catching are two basic handball techniques which must be trained and improved continuously. These 60 practical exercises offer you various options to train passing and catching in a challenging and diverse manner. The exercises particularly focus on improving passing and catching skills even during highly dynamic movements. The drills therefore combine new running paths and movements similar to real game situations.

The exercises are illustrated and described in an easy, comprehensible manner. They can be immediately integrated in every training unit. Various difficulty and complexity levels allow for adjustment of the passing and catching drills to each age group.

Effective goalkeeper warm-up shooting – 60 exercises for every handball unit

Goalkeeper warm-up shooting is essential for almost every training unit. These 60 warm-up shooting exercises provide you with a variety of ideas to make the warm-up shooting challenging and diverse, both for the goalkeepers and the field players. The exercises particularly focus on improving the players' dynamics even during the warm-up shooting.

The exercises are illustrated and described in an easy, comprehensible manner. They can be immediately integrated in every training unit. Whether you combine the exercises with additional coordination drills or use them as an introduction to the main part – various difficulty levels allow for adjustment of the warm-up shooting to each training unit and age group.

Competitive games for your everyday handball training – 60 exercises for each age-group
Handball needs quick and correct decisions in each game situation. This can be trained playfully and diversely through handball-specific games. These 60 exercises are divided into seven categories and train the playing skills.

The book deals with the following subjects:
- Team ball variants
- Team play with different targets
- Tag games
- Sprint and relay race games
- Ball throwing and transportation games
- Games from other types of sports
- Complex closing game variants

The exercises are illustrated and described in an easy, comprehensible manner. They can be immediately integrated in every training unit. Various difficulty levels, additional notes, and possible variations allow for adjustment to each age group.

Paperback from the Handball Practice series (Handball Praxis) (five training units each)

Handball Practice 11 - Extensive and diverse athletics training

Handball Practice 14 - Interaction of back position players with the pivot – Shifting, Screening, and Using the Russian Screen

Special Handball Practice 1 - Step-by-step training of a 3-2-1 defense system

Special Handball Practice 2 - Step-by-step training of successful offense strategies against the 6-0 defense system

For further reference and e-books visit us at:
www.handball-uebungen.de